Contents

Whites & Creams

WHITE IS THE MOST CLASSIC BRIDAL COLOR, AND A WARM PALETTE CAN BE CREATED WITH THE ADDITION OF CREAMS AND IVORIES, WHICH ALSO GIVE BOUQUETS GREATER DEPTH.

The marriage of Queen Victoria and Prince Albert in 1840 is credited with starting the tradition of white weddings, with her satin bridal gown trimmed in white Devon lace and her veil held in place with a wreath of orange-flower blossoms. While there are exceptions, the majority of traditional Western weddings today still favor white and cream hues for bridal gowns and flowers. White remains the emblem of purity and unblemished love.

Stephanotises and certain rose varieties offer some of the purest white hues found in flowers, and *Stephanotis* blossoms have an ideal structure for accenting with pearls or jewels. Lush greens provide a pristine background for white flowers. A purse accented with a *Verbascum* leaf adds whimsy to a cluster of classic blossoms *(opposite, lower right)*.

A traditional white bridal flower is lily-of-the-valley, which pairs perfectly with other springtime blossoms such as tulips, hyacinths, lilacs and *Ornithogalums*. When lilies-of-the-valley or other specialty flowers are unavailable or too costly, some high-quality fabric versions can be tucked among fresh blossoms and go nearly undetected.

❦

White *Cattleya* and
Phalaenopsis orchids are
showstoppers on their own
and add drama to any
bouquet. Fragrant *Gardenias*
(top right), another favorite
white wedding flower,
highlight a cascade of salal
leaves lightly attached to
bullion wire.

❦

For autumn and winter, creamy white flowers blend beautifully with cones, pods, feathers, leaves and burlap for warm wedding presentations. Textural contrasts and distinctive shapes add interest to these fall favorites.

Pinks & Fuchsias

THE RANGE OF PINK HUES MOVES FROM PETAL SOFT TO PINKY
PEACH TO PASSIONATE FUCHSIA — AND EVERYTHING IN BETWEEN.

Pink is a favorite color of many brides whether they
want a soft romantic theme or a fiery passionate ambiance.
Sweet or sassy, there is a pink color combination to match
every mood. Both light and dark pinks can be mingled
successfully with burgundy and blue-violet flowers for a
rich wintery combination or cream and white blossoms for
a lighter mood.

Almost every flower type is offered in tonal pinks, so
bouquets can be fashioned to fit virtually any theme or
price range. From exotic orchids and lilies to romantic roses
and *Ranunculi,* there is an array of pink floral combinations
available to fulfill every bride's dream bouquet. Within
this chapter you will find dozens of bouquets created in a
myriad of floral and foliage combinations, all unified with
variations of pink.

From dramatic flair to demure sweetness, these bouquets are lovely examples of the full range of expression that can be achieved with pink-hued florals.

The gorgeous petals of
Oriental lilies *(above)* make
a formal presentation, and
garden roses and heather
create a more relaxed
bouquet *(opposite, top)*. The
tightly massed carnation
nosegay with a satin-
wrapped handle *(opposite,
bottom)* makes a fragrant
and affordable offering.

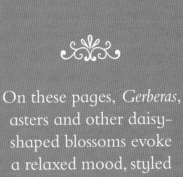

On these pages, *Gerberas*, asters and other daisy-shaped blossoms evoke a relaxed mood, styled alone or combined with other blossoms like roses. Streamers and ribbon-wrapped handles customize bouquets for the bridal party.

This collection of dramatic bouquets shows the versatility of orchids — from a modern cascade of *Cymbidium* orchids *(opposite, left)* to the simple purse enhancement *(opposite, right)*. The exotic combinations of hybrid orchids on this page highlight pink at its most passionate.

The riot of color in these roses and tulips makes a dramatic statement. The multipetaled garden roses are a favorite choice of many brides today. In some bouquets, foliages are as important as the flowers.

Sleek sophistication is achieved on this page with a luxurious cascade of *Dendrobium* orchids *(right)* and a tasseled bouquet of fragrant stock florets *(above)*. The bouquets *(opposite)* show a variety of favorite styles.

With the intensity of color, these bouquets are a blend of romance and regalness. The lily-and-rose bouquet *(left)* is accented with hanging *Amaranthus*. The velvety collar on the bouquet *(below)* is made by gluing petals from *Protea* blossoms to a cardboard circle. Garden roses are featured on the opposite page.

45

Peaches & Apricots

SWEET BUT SOPHISTICATED, PEACH COMBINES BEAUTIFULLY
WITH MYRIAD OTHER COLORS AND IS RIPE FOR THE PICKING IN
MANY WEDDINGS TODAY.

Peaches-and-cream is a popular wedding color combination
that is soft and flattering, with many bridal gowns having a
whisper of peach in the undertones. There are many tints, tones
and shades of peach, from a pale shell-like peach to a vivid
coral, but all are versions of orange. For a pinker peach, a bit
of red is added. Whether a wedding is casual or classic, a wide
range of peach-hued flowers is available to accessorize the
bridal party.

Roses in softer hues of peach are selected for these three wedding bouquets, each with a slightly different composition. Note how the color of ribbon used influences the vividness of the bouquet.

Two bouquets created with similar circular styles *(above and opposite, bottom)* showcase the range of colors and textures available in peach tones. The brighter *Mokara* orchids and *Hypericum* berries *(opposite)* provide vibrancy to the classic roses and carnations, in contrast to the peaches-and-cream look achieved in the all-rose bouquet *(above)*. A spectacular duchess rose *(opposite, top left)* is created with multiple petals from peach-colored roses.

The versatility of peach-colored flowers is evident in this collection. A sheaf of grasses and feathers provides an autumnal tone *(opposite, top)* while shells in the two bouquets above help evoke a beachy sentiment. Deep-toned *Galax* leaves *(opposite, bottom)* or a sophisticated black bag *(left)* offer depth to the soft-hued flowers.

Oranges & Rusts

VIBRANT ORANGE IS A SEASONLESS COLOR FOR WEDDINGS, BUT ADDING A WARM PALETTE OF RUST AND TERRA COTTA TO THE FLORAL MIX GIVES A DISTINCT FEELING THAT FALL IS IN THE AIR.

Orange is the color of adventure and optimism, and it adds visual excitement to wedding bouquets. In the past, orange has been underused in wedding work, but it has become a more popular choice because of its cheerfulness and impulsive edge. In the spring and summer, orange flowers such as tulips, *Gerberas* and poppies can evoke an informal casualness. But as autumn approaches, mix orange flowers with the deeper-toned botanicals of rust and brown with cones, pods, leaves, grasses and feathers.

Roses, *Gerberas* and *Ranunculi* are frequently combined in wedding work and can be fashioned into a variety of bouquet styles. Create armatures with copper wire *(above)* or willow branches *(opposite, top)* for two distinctly different presentations. For a feminine look, soften orange roses with white organza ribbons and a cascade of fabric petals *(opposite, bottom left)*.

A few orange roses, topping off a flange of calla spathes, combine with yarrow and *Leucadendrons* to make a unique small bouquet *(below)*. Waxy white *Stephanotises* are a bright contrast to orange blossoms *(opposite, top and bottom left)*. Baskets and bows *(opposite, far right)* demonstrate how flamboyant orange flowers can take on a casual air.

Fabric monarch butterflies flutter through the cascade of orange *Ranunculi* and white *Phalaenopsis* orchids *(opposite, left)*. A mound of *Gypsophila* makes the base for randomly glued *Gerbera* petals *(opposite, top right)*. And craft mesh forms a collar for this modern "tornado" design and becomes a swirled conical handle when bound with copper wire *(opposite, bottom right)*.

The vibrancy of orange is never more evident than in these bouquets. Graceful *Gloriosas* are featured on this page, one with a woven grassy handle *(above)* and the other combined with *Cymbidium* and miniature *Cattleya* orchids designed atop an elongated handle trimmed with heather. Similar brightly hued flowers are used to create the designs on the opposite page.

Bicolor tulips *(right)* are gathered casually and bound with wide striped ribbon. Terra-cotta and pink roses *(below)* are complemented with *Hypericum* berries and collared with velvety fabric leaves.

Orange roses take on varied looks on the opposite page. Neatly trimmed myrtle *(opposite, bottom left)* surrounds a clutch of orange roses while plaid ribbon and *Magnolia* leaves lend a fall motif to similar blossoms *(opposite, top right)*. Orange and white roses accent a purse for a mother of the bride *(opposite, top left)*.

Finally, orange comes full circle to combine with rust, green and brown for a decidedly fall influence. Deep-toned *Cymbidium* orchids *(right)* are lovely and long lasting. A fabric bouquet holder *(above)* is topped with roses, feathers, leaves, grains and *Hypericum* berries.

A ring of *Hypericum* berries surrounds a simple nosegay of fall-hued daisy chrysanthemums *(opposite, bottom left)*. In fact, *Hypericum* in various hues is tucked into almost all of these bouquets with warm results.

Reds & Burgundies

RED IS A BOLD BRIDAL HUE THAT DEMANDS ATTENTION, BUT IT CAN BE TRANSFORMED FROM DARING TO DEMURE DEPENDING ON HOW IT IS UNITED WITH OTHER COLORS AND TEXTURES.

Red is *the* color of the holiday season, with its varied Christmastime traditions from rich, burgundy velvet gowns to jolly holly berries. It can, however, span the seasons and combine with the rusty-orange colors of autumn leaves or add depth to the lighter tones of summery pinks. Today, flowers of all types, from springtime's vibrant tulips to the classic flower of love, the red rose, are available in varying shades of red.

These ruby red wedding bouquets all appear to have been freshly picked from the garden. The top left design shows garden roses and *Ranunculi* encircled with jasmine vine while crimson *Bouvardia* and variegated foliages provide texture to the bouquet at left. The small clutch shown above is perfect for a mother to carry.

Red roses can move from the classic bouquets found on the next pages to a more high-fashion look shown here. Ideas include a foliage orb to hold in one's hands *(opposite, top)*, glossy feathers *(opposite, bottom)*, specialty handle treatments and a basic bag on this page. There is nothing mundane about these creative bouquets.

A mass of ruffly carnations *(above)* makes a fragrant and inexpensive bouquet while a reptile-patterned backing and coiled fern shoots ("fiddleheads") give a modern theme to a coordinating bouquet and boutonniere *(opposite, top)* At the bottom are examples of reds being softened or brightened, depending on their companion flowers.

Here, a red theme is redefined with a variety of flowers, colors and textures. Trailing ivy *(left)*, downy feathers *(below)* and *Hypericum* berries *(opposite, top)* add unique properties. A floral "rapier" of fresh heather encompasses cherry-tipped carnations in a bouquet fit for a medieval princess *(opposite, bottom right)*.

Yellows & Greens

YELLOW HUES BRING A SUNNY AND JOYFUL AMBIANCE TO WEDDINGS WHILE VERDANT GREENS COMMUNICATE THE RENEWAL OF NATURE.

The color of the summer sun, yellow is the ultimate expression of happiness in a wedding bouquet. Yellow flowers can perform in any season, beginning with spring's daffodils and tulips and then moving to summer's golden sunflowers. Autumn provides us with *Dahlias* and *Chrysanthemums* while winter's flowers include callas and orchids. Creamy-toned yellow blossoms can add softness to almost any bouquet.

Green is the Earth's symbol of renewed growth. From the first blade of grass or tender snowdrop, green signifies new life. Green is no longer relegated only to foliages and accessories; hybridizers have been busy developing green flowers in almost every category, from roses and orchids to callas and carnations. In this chapter, there are some interesting foliage treatments that transform leaves and berries into works of art.

This collection of yellow bouquets sings springtime, with a proliferation of tulips and daisies selected for the designs. From classic round clutches and a simple cascade *(opposite, bottom right)* to an umbrella-style hand-tied *(above)*, these bouquets provide sunshine to any wedding.

Daffodils, tulips and *Ranunculi* combine beautifully for springtime collections. Special ribbon treatments *(opposite)* add elegance to simple hand-tied bouquets and provide a comfortable place for brides to hold the bouquets.

Chartreuse green hues, found in many *Cymbidium* orchids, blend with a wide range of other colors. *Cymbidiums* are long-lasting blossoms that fill space easily and can survive a sunny outdoor wedding.

Small clusters of *Dendrobium* orchids *(opposite, top left)* are bound with decorative wire and combined with green-edged roses for a bright, modern look.

Maidenhair ferns *(opposite, bottom right)*, white miniature *Hydrangeas* and tiny gold ornaments combine to create an airy bouquet.

This collection of green-and-white designs shows more examples of modern wedding work. A ring-bearer pillow *(opposite, bottom left)* is crafted of woven lily grass *(Liriope)*, with a *Hypericum* bow and small nest. A hand-tied bouquet *(opposite, bottom right)* is finished with burlap, and dried wheat collars a mixed bouquet *(right)*. A single specimen orchid is featured in a foliage-and-twig-covered orb *(opposite, top left)*.

Violets & Blues

THE RANGE OF FLOWERS IN VIOLETS AND BLUES OFFERS A BOUNTY OF OPTIONS FOR WEDDINGS, AND THESE COLORS CAN SPAN THE SEASONS DEPENDING ON THE DEPTH OF THE HUE.

Blue is the color of trust and responsibility. Lavender symbolizes refinement and elegance. Purple is regal and aristocratic. Because the availability of true blue flowers is somewhat limited, blues are often combined with the softer lavenders to create romantic color harmonies. When blues are combined with orange or yellow flowers, more vibrant harmonies result. Purple is frequently selected for winter weddings, but it also is a popular choice for combining with flowers in autumn hues. As evidenced on the adjacent page, floral bouquets in these color medleys are versatile and appealing.

A bouquet of stock florets with flower-shaped buttons *(left)* or *Alstroemeria* blossoms rimmed with heather and rosemary *(below)* make affordable options. Lavender roses blend beautifully with many flowers, including fringed tulips, asters and waxflowers.

Pops of fuchsia give lavender a summery quality in these pretty examples. Roses and orchids blend with miniature callas, sweet peas, globe amaranths and stocks while heather rims a fan, and assorted foliages provide accents.

When the bridesmaids' dresses are lavender, these softer-colored bouquets create a lovely contrast. This page features a creamy duchess rose, an orb of *Hydrangea* blossoms and *Ranunculi*, and a hand-tied bouquet with lavender ribbon. The opposite page showcases garden roses with lamb's-ears foliage and a mixed bouquet encircled with variegated ivy.

The casual textures of straw and burlap create country charm when combined with roses, *Lisianthuses* and chrysanthemums. Lily grass adds spontaneity to a short cascade of roses, carnations and orchids *(opposite, top right)*, and the undersides of tulip *Anthuriums* provide a translucent collar to lavender roses and accent flowers *(opposite, bottom right)*. On this page, *Dietes* foliage (*Iris* grass) is woven to form a green mat that encircles a bunch of purple *Irises (right)*, and blossoms of *Agapanthuses* and fragrant *Freesias* form a classic circular bouquet *(above)*.

Dried lavender encircles a single white *Hydrangea* with pearl accents *(right)* while a flower girl bouquet *(below)* is constructed from *Freesias*, 'Paper-white' *Narcissi* and statice. Two summer sheaf bouquets *(opposite, bottom)* contain larkspurs, *Delphiniums*, roses, *Scabiosas*, and assorted grasses and foliages. By contrast, no foliage is used in the tight clutch bouquet of roses, tulips, *Lisianthuses* and *Irises* *(opposite, top)*.

Five bouquet styles are represented on these pages, from a loosely constructed hand-tied bouquet of larkspurs, peonies, *Astilbe*, *Boronia* and *Leptospermum (above)* to a neatly trimmed cascade of *Scabiosas, Delphiniums* and *Guichenotia (opposite, bottom left)*.

Fittonia foliage accents the roses, miniature callas, *Ageratum* and artichokes in the tussie-mussie bouquet *(right)*.

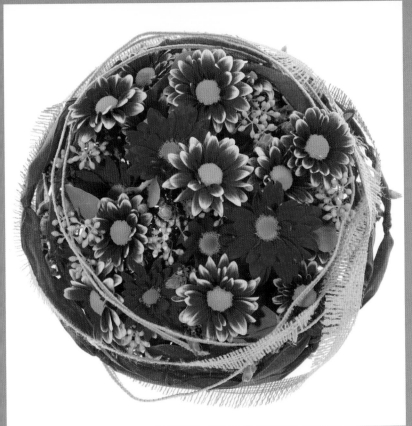

A monochromatic nosegay *(above)* is given dimension with strands of hyacinth florets attached to silver bullion wire. Fragile pansies *(opposite)* are rare components of bridal work but can be incorporated with careful conditioning or, perhaps, using silk or preserved blossoms to tuck among the fresh blooms. Sturdy carnations create a practical and pretty background.

Blue *Muscari* blooms blend with *Stephanotises* in the bouquet above, which incorporates a single white *Hydrangea* as a base. The bouquets on the opposite page feature *Delphinium* blooms as accents to the multicolored bouquets. The conical bouquet *(left)* is created by covering a plastic-foam cone with *Dietes* foliage (*Iris* grass) and attaching a floral-foam cage on top to hold the fresh roses and *Eryngium* blossoms.

Blue *Delphinium* florets are highlighted with *Stephanotises* in the bouquet *(left)* and *Phalaenopsis* orchids on the purse *(opposite, top right)*. Other images demonstrate how bright blue *Hydrangea* florets can be glued to various surfaces for a splash of intense color. *Magnolia* leaves, lilies and hyacinths combine for a striking blue-and-orange combination *(below)*.

Credits

florists'review

PRESIDENT/PUBLISHER: Travis Rigby
EDITORIAL DIRECTOR: David Coake
COPY EDITOR: Fatima Oubaid
CREATIVE COORDINATOR: Lori McNorton
ART DIRECTOR: Mikell Burr
GRAPHIC DESIGNER: Michelle Houlgrave
PRODUCTION COORDINATOR: Cynthia McGowan

*Wedding Collections: Hundreds of Bridal Florals in Seven
Color Palettes* was designed and produced by WildFlower
Media Inc; Topeka, Kansas; *www.floristsreview.com*.

Printed in China

ISBN: 978-0-9854743-7-9

Florists' Review is the only independent trade magazine for
professional florists in the United States. In addition to serving
the needs of retail florists through its monthly publication,
Florists' Review has an active book division that supplies
educational products to all who are interested in floral design.
For more information, visit *www.floristsreview.com* or call
(800) 367-4708.

The creative team at Florists' Review

presents the color groupings and modern designs
today's bridal clients want. *Wedding Collections* will
inspire both you and your customers and make the
planning and sales process easier for all.

WWW.FLORISTSREVIEW.COM

U.S. Retail $24.95

ISBN 978-0-9854743-7-9
52495
9 780985 474379